WAGONS WEST

TRAIL TALES

1848

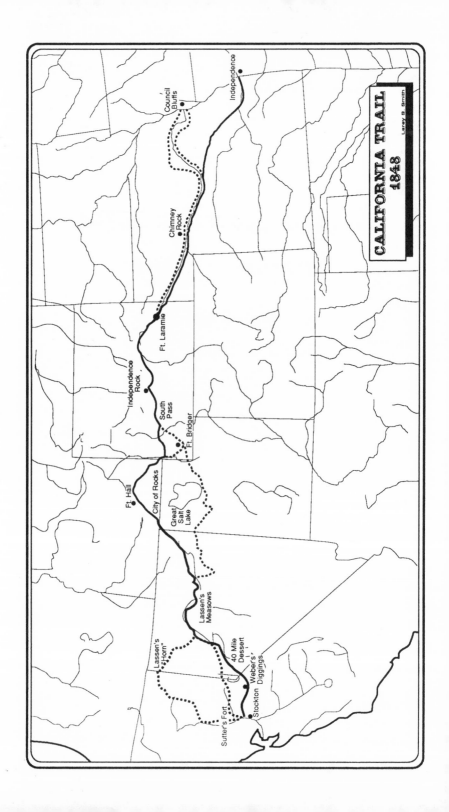

CALIFORNIA TRAIL
1848

Laray S. Smith

Independence

Council Bluffs

Chimney Rock

Ft. Laramie

Independence Rock

South Pass

Ft. Bridger

City of Rocks

Ft. Hall

Great Salt Lake

Lassen's Meaows

Lassen's "Horn"

40 Mile Dessert

Weber's Diggings

Sutter's Fort

Stockton

WAGONS WEST

TRAIL TALES

1848

by

Robert Shellenberger

with sketches by
Sharon Dell'Osso

HERITAGE WEST BOOKS
Stockton, California

1991 First Printing
1996 Second Printing -
A California Sesquicentennial Edition

Cover design by AR Design
                    Stockton, California
Cover Illustration courtesy of Hugh Hays
Sketches by Sharon Dell'Osso
Map by Larey Smith
Layout by Lydia Kim

Published by HERITAGE WEST BOOKS
                    306 Regent Court
                    Stockton, California 95204

————————————

Library of Congress Catalog Number 91-72903

ISBN 0-9623048-3-2

For Alice

FOREWORD

"Moving West" and "Pioneering" are words special to the American story. They shaped our character for the first 250 years of our experience as a people. How can you make a man a peon or a serf if he can pick up and move to new land of his own whenever he feels he has been subject to political, social, or economic abuse? Shoot, he may move "just for the hell of it!" Our geography made the free spirit Yankee psyche unique to the world. (It was often a cruel and irresponsible spirit too, ask any Indian or Passenger Pigeon).

It was nearly always a wagon journey. From New England to Ohio, from The Carolinas to Kentucky, from Indiana to Illinois, it was customarily the family unit moving on by wagon, although some traveled by water and I have read a wonderful account of moving from New York to Ohio in the winter of 1812 by ox-drawn sledge.

The Missouri stretched the tradition to its limits. From here, the move West required months, not weeks, and covered two thousand miles, not tens or even hundreds. These treks were minor epics that fascinate us to this day and continue to inspire writers, painters, and film makers.

It must be noted that the demographics of the frontier are a factor in the early history of the trail. This population included no Hispanics or Asians and only a few free Blacks. There was certainly a Black presence on the frontier—Mountain Man Jim Beckwourth being an eminent example—but they are seldom noted in the early annals of the trail. There *is* occasional reference to families with slaves. The happy aspect of this situation is that it was the usual—but not universal—practice to set slaves free at the end of the journey in California, where slavery was illegal under Mexican law.

This book is an accident. It started when I agreed to provide some short historical items for the newsletter of Stockton's *Yosemite Club*, then approaching its centennial. Stumped for a topic one late evening, I considered the California Trail. Being a "rut nut", I hoped a few items might prove both easy to do and interesting to the readers.

The exercise started as a three or four part series explaining a little of what trail life was *really* like. It was not anticipated we would follow the entire trail. I figured we would "see the Elephant" of boredom soon enough and go on to other matters historical. But the series generated a spirit of its own and became a happy chore, reluctantly concluded after more than thirty episodes.

It was written from general knowledge over a period of about thirty-six months, each episode no doubt influenced by whatever I had read most recently. Though there are absolutely no scholarly pretensions, the series was picked up by the *News and Notes* newsletter of the *San Joaquin County Historical Society*. Interest in the series persuaded *Heritage West Books* to publish the collection.

May the reader also find *Wagons West!* a "happy chore".

Bob Shellenberger
July 1991

TABLE OF CONTENTS

GOING WEST – WHY?

Between 1841 and—say—1868, as many as 350,000 people moved west to California and Oregon. Throw in the late movement to Montana, Idaho, and Colorado and the figure exceeds a half million. Most of them went overland by wagon train. This represents a huge migration, one of the largest voluntary migrations in history in terms of percentages. There were very few people in the whole of the United States who did not know at least one family who had pulled up stakes and moved west.

Why did they go? After all, on a personal basis, it meant abandoning family, friends, position, perhaps forever. On an economic basis it meant selling or abandoning any real estate you owned and reducing your worldly goods to what you could carry in a wagon or two. And it meant an absolutely unknown future. The early leavers in particular, had no idea what they would find when their journey ended.

The frontier had crept from the Atlantic Coast to the Mississippi River in easy stages over a period of two hundred years, and then suddenly stopped. Part of the *American Mystique* had always been to move to the frontier, always in hope of a better farm, a better life. Pioneering was a way of life for many.

The area east to the Mississippi was once one of the world's great hardwood forests, and pioneering had meant clearing the trees before you could farm. At the Missouri River, the trees stopped and the Great Plains began. The old-timers were suspicious of any land where there were no trees to cut down. So, they hesitated. And while they hesitated, the Indians made the plains their own and the federal government decided to leave the plains to the Indians and discourage settlement. So, the pressure grew.

Economics was always a factor. Most people had barely enough worldly goods to fill a wagon. By our standards, they were dirt poor. These were the times when a man wrote a will just to dispose of his feather bed. A crop failure on a subsistence farm really left you with nothing. It was no sacrifice to sell or abandon your home and move on. Some folks ran away from slavery and competition with slave labor.

Perhaps the single most important reason people kept moving west was the search for a healthful climate. Most of the migrants during the forties and fifties came from the border states or those nearby. Hard to believe today, but when originally settled, they were swampy. The one chronic disease almost everyone suffered from was "The Ague." We call it Malaria. Almost everyone suffered episodes of chills and fever. The death rate in isolated farms and villages was terrible, particularly among infants and children. Everyone wanted to move away from areas with a history of "The Ague."

Asian Cholera was another scourge. It came north in waves from the south. In 1850 it was reported that 4,000 people died of cholera in St. Louis alone. That is hard to imagine, in such a sparse frontier population. A lot of folks in Missouri decided to go west that year.

The Romance of Adventure was a bigger factor than we may realize. The people of the Donner Party, for example, were not poor, not ill. In fact, the Donner brothers were conservative, middle-aged Dutch farmers of some standing. Why give it up and move to the unknown? If we have to ask, I guess we will not understand.

The migration began as a trickle to Oregon. The Gold Rush proved the catalyst. The pent-up demand of a generation without a frontier to conquer, suffering illness, bad economic times, and the need to find adventure, now had a target! The migration was on, and it left a heritage that is unique to America. In four months of travel and hardship, these pioneers went twice the distance it took their forebears two hundred years to cover. Wagons Ho!

CHOOSING A RIG

So, here it is 1848 and we have had our fill of rocks and stumps and ague and we want to move on, go pioneering again. Now that the war with Mexico is over, California is the beacon and we can hardly wait to begin our journey.

Our first decision is on how we want to travel. The practical choices are pack train or wagon. The two-wheel ox cart is not a choice for California, although loss of livestock forced more than a few to cut their wagons in half and continue with two wheels and a single yoke. The Mormons were forced to use hand carts for part of their migration to Utah, but that was not an alternative for California or Oregon.

The pack train has the advantage of speed. You can save thirty days. It does not require you "make road" and fording streams and rivers is easier. But it is hard work. All the animals have to be rounded up and packed each day and then unpacked each night. You have no shelter from the elements, and worst of all, if you fall ill or are injured, you probably will be left behind. As one historian has noted, there was not a humane alternative. Pack trains are for sturdy and daring young men.

The wagon is slow, cumbersome, and subject to break downs. But it is a home on wheels. It can give protection from the weather, it stays packed, it can be a fort, and you can carry more — including the sick and the disabled. It is the only choice for a family.

Selecting a wagon is not difficult. The one most often used in the early years is generally called a "one horse" or "two horse" farm wagon. The wagon box is about four feet wide and nine or ten feet long by about two feet deep. It can normally hold about three quarters of a ton—the same as a pick-up truck. You attach a half dozen hickory slats to one side and bend them over to the other. Over this frame you place your canvas top, with a flap in front and a "pucker string" in the back. (Sometimes this cover can cost more than the wagon!).

You want the box to be waterproof, so you will calk it, cover it with canvas or, perhaps, with hides. The top has to be weather proofed and the usual practice is to paint the canvas. Many outfits paint their wagons to match, making a pretty colorful picture when they first jump off. Linseed oil is a standard weather proofing, and for the patient, rubbing your canvas top with bees wax is also a good solution.

The famous Conestoga wagon is used rarely, and

never in the early years. It is too big and too expensive. It is built for hauling tons of freight over regular roads, not for pioneering and pulling across the desert.

The so-called "Prairie Schooner" is larger than a farm wagon—normally carries a ton and a half or more. It features front and rear boards that slope up at an angle, similar to the Conestoga. This gives them a distinctive look, especially after they get their canvas top. We will see some bigger wagons, but they will be trouble. Not many will make it through during the early years of the trail.

Originality is part of the American Character, and as time allows, some modifications are made. One popular adaptation is a false floor that really makes it a two-decker. Gear went below, living and riding accommodations above. Living space is only feasible if you have more than one wagon. If you travel by single wagon, *all* the space is required for food and gear.

We want our wagon "light, but strong." This means compromise. An unbreakable wagon would be too heavy. Seven kinds of wood go into a good wagon, along with some iron reinforcing. It is more sophisticated than you might think. Tongues and axle trees may break and will be replaced with what can be found on the trail. Iron tires will have to be heated and reset along the way, but wheels usually hold up.

A good farm wagon can do the job.

HORSES, MULES, OR OXEN

We splurged and bought a new wagon. It is just a one-horse farm wagon, but it is light and tough and a fine example of the wagon builder's and wheelwright's art. It's a vehicle as common as old boots, but it is new and shiny and it is going to take us to "Californy," (unless we change our minds along the way and split off for Oregon).

We've painted her blue and bought a new canvas top that we have spent many hours rubbing with bees wax. All the wheels and fittings are greased and we have a "tar bucket" full of tallow hanging at the rear to treat a squeaking wheel as may be necessary.

The next step is to choose between horses, mules, or oxen. Horses are not recommended. They are just not rugged enough for the journey ahead. They are stronger, smarter, much faster, but they do not endure without supplemental feed. Our animals are going to have to live off the land, so we will take our saddle horse, but trust our wagon to something more reliable, something that doesn't need grain to fuel itself.

Mules aren't a bad choice. We can get the big Missouri mules that are available on the frontier, or the tough, little Spanish mules up from the Sante Fe Trail. Mules are faster than oxen, don't get sore feet, and can survive on a diet that would give a camel a belly ache. But, they are expensive.

Oxen are slow and cheap. They are generally docile, but do tend to stampede at night. Indians love to steal and eat them, but they do better in the mud. (Incidentally, "oxen" is a term we don't hear any more, because we no longer use them as draft animals. Today we call them steers and send them to the feed lot). Price and reliability convince us, and we buy eight head. We will put three teams in the yokes to pull our wagon—forget that "one horse" stuff—and trail two as spares. Since the children are small, we also buy a fresh "milch cow." That will give us milk and butter along the trail. Along with our saddle horse, we are in better shape than most who only have a single wagon.

The only thing we might add is the family dog. Lots of dogs make the trip, and probably cause more fights and stampedes than the Indians. But, old Prince is a pet, isn't he?

Our traveling rig is now complete. Figuring a ten-foot wagon and ten to twelve feet to each span of oxen, we are in command of a prairie schooner that is between forty and fifty feet long! No reins or bull whips, just trudging along side of them for about 2,000 miles hollering "gee," "haw," "giddy-up," and "whoa." The best is yet to come!

LOAD 'ER UP !!!

This is an exciting time for us. First we decided to make the big move and go pioneering—all the way to California! We have said good-bye to family and friends (also to hard times, we hope), and made our way to Independence, Missouri. We bought a new wagon and covered it with canvas (which is why we call them "covered wagons," if you hadn't thought of it before), and the wife is busy sewing little pockets to the canvas on the inside to keep "handy things handy." We have decided to go with oxen and we are busy trying to gentle them before we jump off. And we have a milk cow, a horse, and Prince, the family dog.

We go shopping for supplies. Our wagon is only about as big as the bed of a pick-up truck, but we will overload her with nearly 2,500 pounds of gear supplies, furniture and most of our belongings.

Flour will be our first item. Probably about 800 pounds—200 pounds for each of us. Bacon will be next.

By "bacon" we don't mean just sowbelly, but any kind of salted or smoked pork. Then some dried beef and fish. A barrel of corn meal in which we will stow as many fresh eggs as possible. We'll eat a lot of eggs until they are either gone or go bad. To this we'll add some beans, rice, lots of coffee, tea, maple sugar, spices, and any home preserves we still have. Pickles will be a big item. We need them to prevent scurvy. And finally, treat of all treats, dried fruit. On some special occasion on the trail—maybe the Fourth of July—we'll have dried apple pie!

We need to milk the cow twice a day. Along the trail, we will hang the morning milk in a covered bucket at the end of the wagon. By night fall, the bumps of the trail will have turned it into sweet butter milk and fresh butter.

One thing we won't take is a big water barrel tied to the side. That would be an ox killer.

By now our wagon is pretty heavy. To this we will add our tent, tools, lead and powder for our fire arms, dishes, pots and pans, a cook stove with a couple of lengths of stove pipe, clothes, bedding, what few books and personal keepsakes we might have, and those special items of furniture we want to be part of our new home. The little farm wagon also must bear any spare parts we've decided upon and a big chain or rope.

If we were a little more wealthy, we would have a second wagon and hire a driver. Thus we could double our load and add only one more mouth to the number we have to feed along the way. But we aren't well-to-do and have already spent about $500 for wagon, livestock, and supplies, and that is the extent of our poke. We are only average folk, after all.

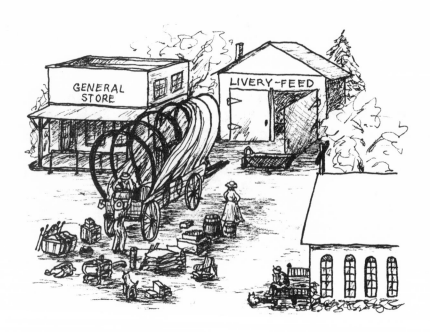

WESTWARD HO !!
WE'RE ON OUR WAY

Jumping off for California in 1848 takes some timing. It depends on Spring grass. We want to leave as early as possible to beat the Sierra snows later on, (the Donner Tragedy, only two years prior, looms large on our mind), but livestock needs grass to survive. It is not until early April we cross the Missouri and fall in with a train still forming. We will travel with them about a week and look each other over. Then we will hold a meeting to elect a captain and write up by-laws (which will soon be broken).

Our route is generally settled, but in 1848 we will still need the experience of a guide. He will cost us about ten dollars per wagon.

As it turns out, only about 100 wagons and maybe 400 people are going to make the trip to California this year. Maybe twice that number are headed for Oregon Territory and we will share the trail with them as far as Idaho. We pick a train to travel with, hoping for a good guide and trustworthy fellow travelers. The latter is chancy—especially in 1848 when the Argonauts seem more motley than usual. One 1850 traveler, Dr. E.A. Tompkins, described his companions in detail in his diary and summed up as follows:

> "A.M. Taylor—a dark hearted demi-devil, W.W. Lapham—a traitorous insidious villain, John Parker—a fitful self sufficient Irishman, A.J. Compton—a pliant would be man..." and of himself, "E.A. Tompkins of whom I will not speak."

Our first week or two help us learn the routine of the trail and how to make camp. First we form a wagon circle, then pitch our tents outside the circle. The horses stay inside the circle if there is enough feed, otherwise they graze with the cattle. We set watches to guard the stock at night,

We become increasingly aware that trees and firewood are far behind us. One of the first things we will chuck from our overloaded wagon is our iron camp stove and the stove pipe. There just isn't wood for it. The youngsters start a daily routine of gathering dry buffalo chips for cooking fires.

We started with six oxen in yokes and two spares for rotation. We soon learn the folly of that idea. Trailing spare steers is no fun and pulling through buffalo wallows and fording creeks and sloughs high with the Spring run-off is tough on our oxen. First chance, we will yoke up our spares.

fourteen

The first few weeks are sobering. Not only do we move out onto the treeless plains, we pass our first graves and cholera is still a peril. We also learn that a little farm wagon with high front wheels and forty feet of teams in front of it does not turn on a dime—in fact it hardly turns at all! We find we do not snake around obstacles, we go through or over them! We are learning to "make road." We have our first midnight stampede of the stock, which is blamed on yapping dogs. There is a meeting on dogs and it is proposed they all be killed. The motion does not carry, but old Prince had better stay close to our wagon and keep his ideas to himself!

Spring storms are also a problem. We cannot sleep in our wagon—it is already full—and our tents are no match for the sudden downpours and high winds that zoom across the prairie. We often sleep wet and cold.

But our spirits remain high, for we are on the trail to California at last!

INDIANS !!!

Going west by wagon train means Indians. Americans have always had an odd love-hate relationship with our original citizens. Their free, natural life-style has always been admired from afar, especially that romantic vision of the Plains Indian in his feathered bonnet, chasing down buffalo, and living under the Big Sky. Up close, attitudes are generally reversed and reflect a dark, unhappy aspect of the American story and the Way West.

In 1848 people are reading Fenimore Cooper's novels and John C. Fremont's reports from the West and generally thrilled at the wild, free life of the Indians of the Plains. Most immigrants have seen "tame" Indians, but yearn to see the real thing—the Wild Indian of the Plains.

Our first meeting is a let-down. Shawnee and Delawares, forcibly transplanted here from the East, know an opportunity when they see it, and operate ferries across the Kansas River to serve the wagon trains. Not what we expected.

Our first six weeks on the trail take us through a corridor that separates Pawnee on the north, from Cheyenne on the south. But, when we get to the upper Platte River, we are in Sioux country. We are of no concern to them now. It will be fifteen or more years before Whites encroach enough to set off the Indian Wars on the Plains. We see them, though, and it is exciting, at least at first. They ride into camp during "nooning" to trade or ask for food. If there are enough of them, they try to bully us into presenting them gifts.

They are often suppliers of meat and game. The farsighted will trade for moccasins for we are using up shoe leather at a great rate.

They can be real pests in camp, poking into everything and prone to steal small objects. They are all infected with vermin and to let an Indian put on your hat is tantamount to making it a gift or subject to trade. You certainly won't wear it again!.

Actually, we are pretty safe if we come across a large party headed by an old Chief. The danger is in being caught out hunting alone by a small party of young men eager to earn their eagle feathers. You can be killed. If you keep your head, you are more likely to be robbed of horse and gun. Sometimes, just for the fun of it, the young braves will strip the lone hunter of all his clothes and send him stepping gingerly back to his train stark naked. Big Joke.

At Fort Laramie we are likely to see a large Sioux camp. Children, especially little blond girls, will be kept in the wagons as we pass by. Some argonauts are convinced the Sioux camped there just to kidnap little blond girls!

Heading over South Pass toward Idaho and Nevada, we will have to be on watch for Sioux, the raiding Crow, and maybe Blackfoot (who are there to raid the Sioux, not us). If we keep a good watch at night, our Indian experience will be interesting but without incident. Little do we realize that the despised "Digger" of the desert, without guns or horses, is going to be our biggest challenge. That adventure is still down the trail.

LIFE ON THE TRAIL

Our year, 1848, is a good year on the trail. Most travelers are heading to the Oregon Territory, but about 100 wagons and 400 people will make it safely to California. Many of the travelers, in contrast to the 49ers who will follow us, are families. Our route is to cross the Plains until we come to the Platte River. We follow the North Fork up past Fort Laramie, up into the high country. We branch off and follow the Sweetwater until we come to South Pass and find ourselves over the Continental Divide.

We are really a moving village. Most of the trains will have left within about 30 days of each other and will meet and pass on the trail several times. After about a month, we will have our routine down, we will have toughened up, and most of the chills and fever of the Ague and the sudden attacks of Asian Cholera will be behind us.

Each morning we rise near dawn, cook a hurried

breakfast while the oxen are yoked, and then move out at a steady two to three miles an hour. We rotate our position in line each day so that each has a turn in the lead and each eats a fair share of dust at the rear. About midday we stop for "nooning". It not only saves us from travel in the heat of the day, it is a vital rest period that allows our livestock several hours of grazing. They are living off the land, and cannot work from dawn to dusk without rest and food.

During the long "nooning" lay-over, the most substantial meal of the day is prepared, clothes darned, harness repaired, tents patched, animals doctored, and—on occasion—clothes washed and even the body bathed. (In one 1850 diary, the record shows it was 30 days before the first clothes were changed and washed and apparently six weeks before the first bath!). Women visit each other and the children play.

Toward mid-afternoon, the stock are hitched up and the trek continues, often until dark or later. Evening means quick meals, taking the stock to feed, and guard duty. Those in camp tell stories, maybe sing along with a fiddle, and then go early to the bedroll.

If it is a very good day, we make twenty-five miles. Twenty miles or less is more usual, since we are using only oxen.

Most of us have never been with so many people at one time. Even when we left our old farm to go for supplies or to church or Fourth of July celebrations, we never saw this many people together in one place before. The children never had so many playmates, the women so many female friends.

Like any typical village, we have our gossips, our feuds, romance and even marriage, and occasional problems of law and order. Alcohol is generally not a problem. We have church services, when we can find a preacher, (we are overwhelmingly Protestant), and many trains will "Keep the Sabbath" by refusing to travel on Sundays. This is not only good theology, it is very good for the animals.

Storm, stampede, illness, mud, dust—all are part of trail life. But on some days, life on the flower-sprinkled prairie does seem like Eden.

TRAIL MISERIES

The first part of the Oregon-California Trail, leading from the Missouri River to South Pass in Wyoming, did not change much over the years. It was originally a trappers' trail to the Rockies. Then the traders discovered they could use the route to take wagons to Rendezvous. In the early 1840s immigrants for Oregon and California just followed in line. From Independence and St. Jo, from Old Fort. Kearny and Council Bluffs, the trail led to and along the Platte River. The south bank was the Oregon Trail, and the north bank from Council Bluffs was the Mormon Trail. The two merged at Fort. Laramie.

Actually, no guide is needed until we get to South Pass. The tracks of the prior year are clear. Beginning in 1849, the trail will became a misery.

Consider 22,500 people and 80,000 animals on the trail in '49. Then, 1850 will *double* the traffic of '49. The trail will actually become ten miles wide in some areas! The wagons and cattle will turn the trail to dust and then to mud during spring rains. Manure of every variety will cover our path. The hot, choking, alkali dust of the high plains will seem half manure.

Animals die almost daily. The first touch of alkali takes its toll and then illness, poor food, bad water, and poor treatment add to the sacrifice. Dead animals will line the trail, putrefying. Any wild game not scared off by this horde of people and animals, are likely to be shot, adding guts and bones to the mix. Tons of spoiled food stuffs will go into the brew that will finally be topped with human waste. You will be able to *smell* your way to the Rockies in '49 and '50.

We all add our share of junk to the trail as we continually jettison plows, anvils, furniture, and spoiling food to lighten the load that is wearing down our animals.

The high plains provide little forage for a mass of animals. Camping will sometimes mean herding the oxen miles to grass that has not already been grazed to the nub. Wagon trains will "race" to known water holes with good feed. One captain rafted his train across a river and then chopped up the raft so as to keep his lead. Trees for another raft might be twenty miles away.

Coming to a clear spring or stream, the people drink first, then the horses, and finally the oxen and steers have their wallow. Hours later the next train will start the sequence all over again. Boiling water for purification is rare and diarrhea is epidemic.

There are no privies on the trail. In camp, privacy by way of trees, rocks, or a ravine is soon sought out for nature's purposes. Trains following will, of course, use the same area rather than despoil another. In time, especially in '49 and 1850, some of these locations will become noteworthy for their stench and flies.

And the human dead. People die every year on the trail—more than 500 in '49 alone—and are hastily buried, only to sometimes be dug up by Indians looking for clothing or, more usually, by wolves and coyotes looking for lunch. Bits and pieces of human bodies will be seen by almost every argonaut of '49 and 1850.

Our year, 1848, might be described as the last "pristine" year. Aren't we glad we missed the "Rush?"

THE LADIES OF THE
TRAIL

The Ladies are *good* at trail travel. Wagon train life agrees with most of them and if they are not as strong as men, they are at least as tough—and better survivors.

Most of the women of the ill-fated Donner Party survived. Most of the men did not. Who can forget Tamsen Donner, who sent her children to safety but refused to leave her dying husband, only to later succumb (and perhaps end in the stew pot), herself?

The Stevens Party of 1844 was the first to get wagons over the Sierra. It was almost totally a family train. Helen Murphy was a member. She rode ahead on horseback to Sutter's Fort with some other young folk. On the way they became the first Europeans to stand on the shores of Lake Tahoe. Upon arrival at Sutter's, Helen met Captain Charles Weber, member of the Bartleson Party of 1841 and later founder of

Stockton, California. They married in 1850 and thus she became Stockton's first "first lady."

The Forty Niners who stumbled into Death Valley in 1849 included four separate families, all of whom got through. If William Lewis Manly was the hero of Death Valley, tiny Julia Brier was the heroine. Her sickly husband was of no use, and 90-pound Julia yoked the oxen, drove the wagon, fed the family, and when they had to abandon their rig, loaded her children onto an ox and led them and her preacher husband to safety. Manly called her *the best man in the outfit.* She died peacefully in 1913 in Lodi, California, aged 99.

The "belle" weather of the astonishing ladies of the trail was a member of the very first overland party of immigrants to head for California, the Bartleson Party of 1841. She was Nancy Kelsey, only eighteen years old. Later in life she told a reporter, *"Where my husband goes, I go. I can better endure the hardships of the journey, than the anxieties for an absent husband."* The hardships of this journey included abandoning the wagons in the Utah desert and walking barefoot over the Sierras carrying her year-old baby. They barely survived by eating the mules. Joseph Chiles, a member of the party, later wrote, *"She bore the fatigues of the journey with so much heroism, patience, and kindness that there still exists a warmth in every heart for the mother and her child."* Her husband, Benjamin, was one of a large clan of rough frontiersmen who were in frequent trouble with the authorities. Kelseyville in Lake County, California, commemorates the name, but they seemed to have been everywhere in the West.

Remember the story of little America Kelsey? David Kelsey, his wife and eleven-year-old America, attempted to settle in French Camp in 1844. Kelsey fell ill with small pox and his wife loaded her family into a wagon and headed for Sutter's Fort for help. They got no further than McCloud Lake, future site of the Stockton City Hall, where Kelsey died and she also fell ill, blinded by the disease. The two men who lived here abandoned the family as soon as the pox was diagnosed, leaving little America, alone in the wilds with her father dead and unburied, and her blinded mother to nurse until help finally arrived. (Two years later, at the age of thirteen, she married her rescuer!)

But, back to Nancy. Old Ben wandered for twenty more years through Oregon, Texas, and Southern California—Nancy at his side. During her interview, she said:

> *I have enjoyed great riches and suffered the pangs of poverty. I have seen U.S. Grant when he was little known. I have baked bread for General Fremont and talked to Kit Carson. I have run from bear and killed most all other kinds of game.*

A *real* trail lady!

SIGHT SEEING ON THE TRAIL

Life on the trail may have been grim at times and the grit of the argonauts tested beyond their early imaginings, but it was also adventure and it was a chance for some rare fun. In fact, some "pioneers" of 1841—the first to head for California—went only as far as South Pass in the Rockies and then decided it was time to get home to harvest the crops! They had traveled a thousand dangerous miles, apparently for the adventure and to see the sights. (Of course, some of them saw the Elephant!)

The first new experiences included venturing onto the treeless plains, meeting Indians, investigating prairie dog towns, (they fascinated everyone), and giving chase to buffalo. The first landmarks everyone noted in their diaries were Court House Rock and Chimney Rock. The latter is a tall sandstone needle that sticks up from the plains of Nebraska very near the trail and it was almost impossible to resist a jaunt over to the base to inscribe your name or initials. (It is still there, but much shorter today due to weathering).

We can look on the practice of leaving your name on every landmark as just a higher quality of graffiti than we see today, but actually, these opportunities were sought out as a means of reassuring those that might be following that you had at least made it this far. Part of the exercise included scouring these locations in search of some mark that indicated a friend or relative who preceded you was still safe and well when this particular landmark was passed. Then you left your own mark.

The technique for leaving your own mark along the trail varied with trail conditions, the amount of time you could devote to your art work, and the material of your slate. Nearly all the marks that have survived the past hundred thirty or so years are scratched deeply into rock. Some rocks are harder to scratch than others. If time were short, you could paint your name and year. If you didn't have any paint along, you could use axle grease or the goop from your tar bucket. And, not a few used a long stick and that other handy item you might leave plopped along the trail. (These weren't all elegant people, you know!).

At any rate, they left their mark at all the major sights, including Scott's Bluffs, Register Cliffs, Independence Rock, and on into the desert.

Natural phenomena astonished them. Ice Slough in western Wyoming was a big hit. The pioneers usually passed this area in early July. It is high desert that plagued them with heat, dust, alkali, and poor feed. Yet, there was this one place where you could dig a few feet into a muddy stream bottom and come up with ice! Something to write home to the States about.

Continuing west into the desert, they found many hot springs that were always fascinating. They soaked in them, laundered in them, got diarrhea drinking from them; they watched them steam and gurgle and boil and were amazed. Unfortunately, many are now gone due to lower water tables, flood from reservoirs, farming practices, and old age.

The sights were there: snowy peaks in the middle of summer, ice on the bucket in August, new animals such as prairie dogs and mountain sheep and goats, new birds, cactus, and geologic wonders. The travelers enjoyed them all. It was a part of the adventure.

GETTING OUR BEARINGS

Before we continue our 1848 wagon journey, a look at the history of our trail will help us appreciate this legacy.

It was 1841 before anyone tried to take a wagon train to California. Spurred by letters from John Marsh (of Brentwood), fifty people met near Independence, Missouri and tried to decide the best way to get to where no one had gone before in a wagon. Take the Santa Fe Trail and then across to Los Angeles? Just strike out west? A missionary party heading for the disputed Oregon Territory made up their minds. Thus they pioneered the trail up the Platte River and across South Pass. Thirty-three people completed the trek, but their wagons were abandoned in Utah. This was the famous Bartleson Party that included John Bidwell, Captain Charles Weber, Joseph Chiles, and Andrew and Nancy Kelsey.

In 1842 no one made an attempt, but Joseph Chiles

returned east, learning as he traveled. In 1843 he led the second attempt. He piloted his small train as far as Fort Hall, Idaho. Here, short of supplies, he sent his horsemen on by way of Oregon and his wagons down to the Humboldt sink. They got across the desert safely but wandered far south in search of a way through the Sierra. They deserted their wagons near Owens Lake and had to hike all the way to the Coast Range.

In 1844 the Stevens Train made the third try. They had no idea of how Chiles had fared the prior year, but they followed his wagon tracks to the Humboldt sink. Then, instead of following the tracks south, Chief Truckee directed them across the Forty Mile Desert to what is now the Truckee River. From there they tried Donner Pass, but snow prevented a wagon crossing. They left some wagons until spring, when they returned and hauled them over the summit and down to Sutters Fort. It took them two seasons, but the wagons made it and the California Trail was now proved.

In 1845, pioneers began jumping off from St. Joseph. There were a number of parties—all heading for Oregon. No one yet knew about the Steven's success. Along the trail they picked up the news, and many diverted to California, including one party that crossed Donner Pass in December!

The year 1846 was a big year. It was also the year of early winter and the Donner Tragedy. Each year had seen improvements and "cut-offs" along the trail, but the Donner train took two false "cut-offs." They fought their way to Salt Lake and then across the Utah desert by the slowest possible route. Finally trapped by snow at the Sierra lake that would carry their name, this tale of starvation and horror doesn't need retelling here.

No one wanted to go to California in 1847 because of the war with Mexico. Hundreds were on the trail headed for Oregon. This was also the year of the mass Mormon migration to Utah. The trail's east half was busy, but only about 90 wagons went on to California.

So, here we are on the Platte, just past Fort Laramie. The trail is really only four years old and still full of kinks and mysteries, but marked and busy. We will soon reach the first "Parting Of The Ways." What will it be: Oregon? The new settlement of Salt Lake City? Or on to California and the war with Mexico? There is one other possibility. Maybe we have "seen the Elephant" and will turn back for "home." Many did.

OVER THE TOP

It is the end of June and we have traveled a long way. The new green grass of Spring sent us on our way. At first we traveled the flowered prairies, fighting streams, small rivers, sloughs and wallows high with winter run-off. We endured spring thunder storms that stampeded our cattle, blew down our tents, and soaked us through. Our people suffered all the usual wet weather maladies, bouts of the ague, and the fear of virulent cholera that could bury a strong man in a day—or quicker. We have endured broken wagons and broken bones.

When we reached the Platte River the road turned to sand—a tough pull—and we met alkali and poison water for the first time. As we moved into today's Wyoming we were plagued by dust. Not just dust, but alkali dust, as fine as flour. And hordes of mosquitos, often when there didn't seem to be any water to support them. The animals suffer from bad water and poor grazing. We have buried some dead.

But now there is a new life in our legs as we leave the Platte and follow the Sweetwater River higher, gently higher toward the snowy peaked Rockies. We are nearing South Pass, the wagon travelers' remarkably easy passage over the Continental Divide. Maybe we have seen a piece of the Elephant over the last 900 miles, but we ain't beat yet!

We reach Independence Rock very near the Fourth of July (after which it was named). Even in 1848 we find dozens of names painted and scratched on its surface, including mountain men, John C. Fremont, and perhaps members of the Donner Party. Ahead we see Devil's Gate and know we are near.

We will celebrate The Fourth with rifle salutes. Perhaps some oratory and a church service will be provided. If there is a fiddle we will have a dance— quadrilles, mostly. And the ladies will dig into our diminished larder in search of one remaining treat. Remember those dried apples we splurged on back in the States? Well, if we can find a camp oven that hasn't yet been tossed away, we can use the wagon seat to roll out the crust for an apple pie! Independence Day is rarely neglected on the trail.

Why is a pass so far north called "South"? Because it is south of the traditional home of the Indians that named it. Only 7,490 feet high, it provides a wide and gradual route through the heart of North America's mightiest range. The climb is so gradual over the last day's travel that the summit can't be discerned. Confirmation comes only when we note a small stream flowing west. West! West to the Pacific Ocean!

There is no turning back now. We are committed to "go the distance." We are exhilarated. And we are tired. We continue down to Pacific Springs (great name!) and camp in good grass with good water. Tomorrow we will rest to "recruit" our cattle and take stock of our situation.

But look how far we have come!

MEANWHILE, BACK ON THE TRAIL...

At Pacific Springs we rest and "recruit" our animals while we decide what to do next. (Incidentally, next year when the 49ers come through here by the thousands, they will turn this spring into a mucky quagmire with only bad water, little feed and hordes of mosquitos to offer).

A lot is happening that will affect our travels over the next 1,000 miles, and we don't know any of it—yet.

In January, gold was discovered at Sutter's Mill. The news is traveling up the trail toward us. Once we hear of it, there will be no more talk of Oregon!

The famous Mormon Battalion that traveled south to Santa Fe and then across to Los Angeles in the late war with Mexico, is now making its way home to Salt

Lake. Leery of the rough reputation of the Truckee Canyon, they decide to search for an easier way over the Sierras. They pick a ridge to follow, and after the loss of three men to Indians (at Tragedy Springs near Silver Lake in present day Amador County), they pioneer a new route that will become the favorite— The Carson Route, (named after the West Branch of the Carson River, which it follows). As they proceed eastward with their wagons, they will spread the word to the west bound of their new route.

Peter Lassen, the northern California pioneer of only small abilities, is out on the trail trying to entice wagons to come to California via his ranch. He will "lead" the unsuspecting across the Black Rock Desert, to a route he has never traveled! It will become known as "around Lassen's Horn".

Finally, ahead of us on the trail, is a train led by Joseph Chiles, a real veteran now on his fifth trip. When he learns of the Carson River route, he will put his knowledge of local geography to good use. Upon reaching the Humboldt Sink, he won't go west to the Truckee River, but continue south across the Forty Mile Desert, directly to the Carson River, and from there over the new trail. This creates yet another new alternative.

This is only the fifth year the wagon trail has been open. Actually, this portion has been little used and it is changing as we go. We have a lot of alternatives and decisions ahead of us, and this means we will also have more than a few arguments.

But for now, we head down the west slope of the Rockies to Dry Sandy Creek, and then Little Sandy and finally to the first "Parting of the Ways." We can continue southwest to "Fort" Bridger, actually old Jim's trading post, or we can go due west to the Green River. If we go via Bridger's, we will have the possibility of buying additional supplies (at a very high price), and the further alternative of going to newly-founded Salt Lake City. (We also would have to double back north to continue our travel).

The other alternative is called Sublette's Cutoff. It is a tough 45 miles (two days) without water, but felt to be shorter. Bridger offers nothing we can afford, and we are a little uneasy about how we might be treated by the often persecuted Mormons, so it is "Good Bye and Good Luck" to those who go south and "Westward Ho!" for us.

TRAIL LORE

We have taken our little wagon "over the top" and face the challenge of traveling 45 miles to the Green River without feed or water. This means a dry camp tonight. Two months ago this dare might have sent us into a real tizzy, but we are a lot wiser than when we started this trek.

We know the animals can do it—if we don't push them too hard. We know it is smart to cut some hay to take along with us. This helps. Actually, the two days rest at Pacific Springs has helped them a lot. One thing we noticed is that despite all the misery our journey through alkali country caused both man and beast, it did help to heal up their sore hooves.

There are lots of little tricks we never learned back home on the farm. For instance, we gave our wagon a good, tall canvass top to allow plenty of room inside (though you can't sleep in there, what with all the supplies and furniture and stuff). Going west across the prairies into a westerly headwind, that tall top put up so much wind resistance you would think we had added ten tons to the load. (It was also a fierce problem in those terrible spring storms). So, to make some progress and save the animals, at first chance we shortened the hickory slats and lowered our profile.

Watching others taught us another trail-wise trick. Whenever we must ferry or float a river, we take the top all the way off. A canvas top on a windy crossing will inevitably "sail" you into trouble. Those who are stubborn about this point, risk losing wagon and contents to a swift western river. The careless don't realize drowning is a major cause of death on the trail.

We have learned to block up our wagon bed when crossing smaller streams. It's a chore, but the extra inches help keep the contents dry.

The high desert dries out our wooden wagon and wheels. Spokes get loose. Now, when we cross a stream, we try to find time to let the rig soak a little, just to tighten things up.

A covered, loaded wagon has a high center of gravity, so side-hill travel is out. You stay in the swales or follow the ridges. The shortest distance between two points is not always the safest way to travel by wagon.

We have also learned that beans and rice don't cook worth a darn at these Rocky Mountain altitudes. If we have to keep lightening the load, those little sacks of rice and beans will be left by the way-side.

We try to not lay-over at the same camp site for more than a day, because on the second night our grazing stock wanders farther from camp, making it harder to round them up the next day. More than once we have lost up to half a day rounding up lost and strayed stock. It is better to make a small move to new graze.

Water becomes more dear as we roll into ever drier terrain. "Back-East" we would follow a dry creek down stream where it would eventually lead to a stream or creek. In this arid land, we now know you work up-stream in search of pools or springs.

Little things. But, we're learning. And we're getting there!

ANOTHER RIVER TO CROSS

The trip to Green River by way of Sublette's Cutoff is a misery. Dry, tough going the whole fifty miles. We take all the water we dare carry, which is enough for family and our pet dog, and a snuffle for the horse. But the oxen do without. All we can do is "bait" them with the little hay we cut and brought along. One traveler noted there was plenty of water, but it was all in Green River! Great care has to be taken as we near the river on the afternoon of the second day, for when the oxen get scent of the water, they are likely to stampede for the river, dragging the wagons behind like a tail of old shoes.

The snow-fed Green rushes through the high desert on its way to the Colorado and the Pacific Ocean. It is our most dangerous ferry crossing. Most of our ferry crossings were early in the trip. We started with the Missouri, of course, and then the Indians helped us at the Kansas and the Vermillion. We made our own ferry at the Big Blue and the Mormons ferried us across the North Platte. We forded the others, including the South Platte.

The place you first reach the river is not necessarily the safe place to cross. While the oxen rest and recover from their ordeal, we explore for a crossing and hope we find a ferry when we do. If not, we must fell trees and build one.

Sometimes a ferry is just a raft. More often it is built of two big logs in the manner of a catamaran with grooves for the wagon wheels. We pull the wagons across, one at a time, by long ropes. All the animals must swim. Sometimes a traveler who has put together a good ferry and had good luck, will stay behind and operate at a fee for a few days, just to pick up some extra money or barter for some special supplies. Then he will abandon it and rush ahead to his train. Since last season (1847), the Mormons have operated several ferries along the trail, both to help their own immigrants and as a business on behalf of their settlement. Their tolls are generally considered fair and it is an enormous convenience in the wilderness.

Swimming the livestock across is dangerous and has led to many drownings. The cattle first must be coaxed into the swift, cold water where they are prone to balk halfway and turn back, running right over the trailing herders. In one incident in the fifties, a group of Mormon cowboys took a herd of beef cattle across a river only to have them stampeded by barking dogs from a train already across. The herd rushed back into the river and over the cowboys, drowning all fourteen of them.

Most rivers are forded, which is a little safer, but rarely easy. The wagons pitch down the bank, occasionally upsetting, and double teams are often necessary due to the hard pull. The trick is to head slightly downstream until you reach the middle, and then turn slightly upstream. If you do it right, your wagon train forms an arc in the river as you cross.

We hate river crossings, but this is the last tough crossing between us and Sutter's. Tomorrow we cross and head for Fort Hall.

INTERLUDE ON THE TRAIL

W e have just made a safe crossing of the Green River and are pointed northwest toward Fort Hall. This is a minor Hudson's Bay Company outpost. It has been allowed to stay and phase-out over a short period of years under terms of the recent Oregon Territory treaty *("Fifty-four Forty or Fight!")* with England. (If you feel lost, we are leaving today's Wyoming and rolling toward the future site of Pocatello, Idaho).

We still have some rough, dry country to get through and one last touch of alkali (at least for now). We have discovered that some of that dry, white powder along the dry arroyos makes perfect baking soda, so we replenish our supply of that staple. Days are hot, but nights are cold and ice on the buckets is common in the morning in this strange climate. Finally we have wood for our fires again, just as the providential buffalo chips disappear. Too bad most of us have already thrown our iron camp stoves away to lighten our load—an exercise that seems never ending as we continue to litter the trail with anvils, furniture, plows, tools, and less important impedimenta. We are not nearly as sentimental about our goods as we were 1300 long miles back!

Now we travel along the Bear River with good water and ample feed for the stock. Wild berries and greens are available and we find game in the form of deer, antelope, and mountain sheep. We have even discovered a fish new to us, the western rainbow. Our diet has mostly been bacon and bread, bread and bacon. We are beginning to show the first signs of scurvy, and those who will eat what the land provides get a welcome injection of vitamins. Those who don't will pay the price later on the trail or in the Diggings where the diet will again be bacon and bread. We relearn an old lesson—the sudden reintroduction of fresh meat into the diet leads to diarrhea.

We are getting trail worn, but cholera is now behind us and attacks of chills from the ague are less frequent. We feel good, except those down with an attack of fever and welts. We learn at Fort Hall they are suffering from Rocky Mountain Fever—whatever that is.

For the first time since we left the Missouri we see real trees! It occurs to us that except for the cottonwoods and a few willows that grow along the creeks and rivers, we have missed seeing trees. Part of one day the trail actually travels through a small fir forest. We become somber and a little homesick travelling in the shade and quiet, hearing again the sound of the woodpecker and fondly remembering the homey cluck of chickens.

Finally, we reach another trail landmark, Beer Springs. The springs are in two mounds about twenty feet high. The water is good and there are lots of opinions of what it really tastes like, but it sure ain't beer! Steamboat Spring is nearby and we are likely to meet Indians of the Snake Tribe as we approach Fort Hall.

Health, fresh food, good water, good feed, trees, firewood, good weather; we have earned this interlude.

THE TRAIL AND THE ELEPHANT

They say it all started with a joke.

It seems this farmer had all his life wanted to see an elephant. (In the early nineteenth century, isolated and unsophisticated Americans had a yen for the exotic). One day the farmer heard a show was coming to town and that it featured an ELEPHANT! So, Saturday morning he loaded his wagon with all the produce he hoped to sell, dressed in his best, and set off to "see the Elephant." As he approached town, he rounded a corner and his rig came face to face with the ELEPHANT. The horses startled at the sight of the strange beast and ran away, pitching off the farmer and all his goods in the process. Finally they wrecked the wagon, broke loose and ran on until they disappeared. Meanwhile, the farmer ended in the brambles with injury to both his body and his dignity. Friends rushed to his aid and one and all sympathized with his misfortune. He had lost his team, his wagon, his goods. His best suit of clothes was ruined and he was in need of medical aid."Yes," he said, "but at least I got to see The ELEPHANT!"

This knee slapper spread all over the country much as "Kilroy was here" did in World War II. "Seeing The Elephant" became part of western lingo. Pioneering was the hardest kind of life, full of tragedy, setbacks and disappointments. These people loved the irony of the story because it reflected the only attitude that made survival and eventual success possible on the frontier.

The phrase became particularly identified with the early years of the trails west. Pass an abandoned wagon and someone would knowingly say "Well, at least they saw The Elephant." A family would lose mother or father to cholera or livestock to the Indians and reluctantly turn back. They would sheepishly tell their friends upon their return that "We saw The Elephant." "The Elephant" became the embodiment of all the unknown terrors of the trail—cholera, stampede, Indians, flood and drownings, break-downs, accidents, fever, desert, bad water, no water, starvation, dust, alkali....

There was no real shame in seeing The Elephant. It did not have the connotation of cowardice or lack of resolve. It meant simply that you were beaten by something too big for anyone to control.

If you could recover from a major scare or setback

and continue on, you could proudly admit you had seen "a piece of The Elephant." Tough spots on the trail were named after certain parts of the critter—The Elephant's Backbone, The Elephant's Trunk, (and, no doubt, other parts of its anatomy).

During the Gold Rush, the term changed meaning. A man in San Francisco might decide to go try mining and tell his friends he was "off to see The Elephant." Or a miner might make a rich strike and holler "I've found The Elephant!" For some, California was The Elephant.

But, after more than three months and 1300 miles on the trail in this year of 1848, we'll recognize The Elephant if we see it, won't we?

IS THERE A DOCTOR ON THE TRAIL?

Don't even try to imagine what illness, accident, or bad luck may overtake us on the trail. Estimates vary, but a reading of the old diaries suggests anywhere from five to fifteen percent of us will die before we reach California. Most will succumb over the first thousand miles, usually from cholera and the other maladies they bring with them. The last part of the trail will take the biggest toll on animals.

If we are lucky, our train will include a Doctor. The well-rounded Stevens Party of 1844 included a blacksmith, gunsmith, former mountain man, and a doctor among its small party—one reason they were first to get wagons safely to California. In 1849 and 1850 there were so many people on the trail that doctors of a sort were common. But our year is 1848 and we will be lucky if we are ever closer than 600 miles to skilled medical care.

Skill in medicine is problematical in 1848. Doctors come in several varieties. There are allopaths, homeopaths, eclectics, Thomsonians and quacks. The "regular" allopathic doctors from the best schools have a good knowledge of anatomy, a primitive pharmacopoeia, and practice "heroic" medicine that includes bleeding, purging and blistering. Surgery is often still in the realm of the barber.

The gentle homeopath treats you by matching your symptoms. If you have a fever, he will make you sweat even more. If you have diarrhea you get a physic— but usually in small doses. The allopath does just the opposite. If you have a fever he will try to cool you. If you have diarrhea he will try to constipate you. The eclectic tries a little of both. Thomsonians believe in steam heat. Heaven help you if forced to switch from one variety to the other.

Standard remedies include quinine, calomel, and laudanum—none of which require a prescription. Quinine is standard (and appropriate) for treating the ague (actually malaria). Calomel is a mercurial purgative normally administered with cayenne pepper to help things along. It can kill you if it *doesn't* work. Laudanum is a favorite. It is a tincture of opium and not a few get addicted to it. You feel soooo good! There is also an array of salts, salves, liniments, and patented elixirs.

We all have our own remedies, of course. Many of them are interchangeable—good for man or beast! Mostly, we cope by using common sense and our traditional folk medicine.

The common medical problems are diarrhea, dysentery, cholera, typhoid fever, and—of course—bouts of the ague. Late on the journey some suffer scurvy and a few of us picked up Rocky Mountain Spotted Fever, but it will be years and years before there is much help for that!

Accidents take a big toll. Too many guns in the hands of the unskilled wound and kill. Animals injure many. As slow as they are, wagons still crush the careless, especially children. The only treatment for a badly crushed limb is amputation, which is usually followed by infection and death.

Miscarriage and infant death are so common as to barely merit mention.

Unfortunately, science has not yet discovered the connection between bacteria and disease. One diary notes *"...our drinking water is living—that is it is composed of one third fine green moss, one third pollywogs, and one third embryo mosquitoes...."* Water holes and springs are contaminated by each passing train and streams and rivers by waves of buffalo that roil and foul the water. We eat and drink with as much sense as our critters.

Wagon trains are not for the finicky!

FORT HALL

W e have crossed the Rockies, ferried the Green River, and moseyed north toward Fort Hall as we try to rest and recruit our trail-worn animals and recover a little of our own energy. But, we can't poke along for more than a few days. The toughest part of our journey is still ahead—the desert and the Sierra.

We have been looking forward to Fort Hall. It is a chance to get news, make some repairs, buy some supplies (especially flour), and mail letters home to "The States." Each evening we try to write a few lines to family and friends in anticipation of Fort Hall.

Approaching Fort Hall, our hopes begin to fade. It doesn't appear to be as big as Fort Laramie. Hudson Bay people, who own the fort, meet us cordially but they ask us to camp some distance away so to save the pasture near the fort for their stock.

Our long anticipated visit to the fort dashes all our

plans. First, the people at the fort are as anxious to buy supplies from us as we are to buy from them. Supplies come to the fort only by occasional mule train from the Oregon settlements and they are always short on staples themselves. Worst of all, while they agree to take our mail, they point out that it will get through to the States quicker if we carry it on to California. Needless to say, there is no mail for us.

There is no point in staying. We pick up what news and trail lore we can and move on west along the Snake River until it intercepts the Raft River. This is the final "Parting of the Ways." We bid a last good-bye to our Oregon bound trail companions of so many months and turn south toward Nevada. We have shared a lot of adventures and hardships and it is hard to say good-bye—probably forever. But the parting is harder for them than for us, because at Fort Hall we have heard that there is GOLD in California! We are not sure yet whether it is a Humbug or not, but the idea lightens our step as we climb away from the Snake and head out for the Humboldt.

Travel is tough from the beginning with high ridges to cross, followed by steep descents that require we chain up our wheels and even drag logs behind us (our wagons have no brakes). Dust and heat are terrible and water is a constant concern.

Our clothes are shabby and our boots are worn. To save our rundown stock, everyone walks. It is too hot to go barefoot and we wish we had traded more aggressively with the Indians for moccasins back on the Plains. Ladies who insist on shoes instead of boots will wear out twelve pairs between "jumping off" and arrival at Sutter's. You can bet they will save that last pair for journey's end. The word "footsore" is about to take on new meaning.

The Elephant is still out there—maybe closer than ever.

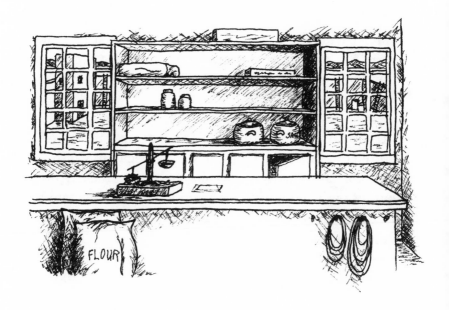

IT'S ALWAYS AUGUST IN NEVADA

There is a cruel twist to the California Trail. No matter when you start, no matter how fast or slow the journey, nearly everyone is destined to cross the Nevada deserts during the hottest, driest month of the year—August.

It is all in the timing. You cannot jump off for California until April or early May because you have to wait for the spring grass for your livestock. And you cannot wait too long before you leave because you must beat the Sierra snow (let's all remember the fate of the Donner Party). So, we are all captive to a four to six week window. Will it be the desert in late July and early August? Mid August? Late August? Take your pick.

To add to the coming misery, we are trail worn. Early on we got toughened up to trail life. However, months of exposure, poor diet, and extraordinary physical effort have taken a sure toll. We are weary. Our animals are weak and dropping off, and our supplies are low. It is hot. Welcome to Nevada!

But the darndest things keep showing up. First we come to a small valley guarded by two large, rock portals that some say look like cathedrals. Everywhere in this small valley are outcroppings of rock, all in strange shapes. It looks like "gnome town." The Argonauts dubbed it "The City of Rocks." All the diaries will mention this bizarre "city."

After a great climb, we come to Thousand Springs Valley. It is true: there are springs everywhere. Hot springs. Cold springs. Tepid springs. For a few days, at least, we have plenty of graze and plenty of good water.

We pick up the Mary's River, a branch of the Humboldt. We will follow the Humboldt across Nevada for the next few weeks and the next several hundred miles. There is grass along the banks if the trains ahead have not grazed it all off. If they have, we will swim the river, cut grass, and float it back for our livestock. The water starts good, but gets worse and worse as we go downstream to where our desert life line will finally disappear into the sands of the sink, leaving us low and dry.

Our spirits and our supplies also "sink."

There is one final twist. We are in the land of the Diggers. We have met the Pawnee, the proud Sioux, the warrior Blackfoot and passed unscathed. But the despised Digger of the desert is about to collect his due.

THE DREADED DIGGERS

Early wagon train folks never know what to make of the desert Indians. They are Utes, Paiutes, Shoshones, and sometimes even Bannocks and Snakes, but the pioneers refer to them all as "diggers" and loathe them completely.

These are the Indians without horses and guns, forced by their enemies to live in the desert. Here they exist in delicate balance with nature, relying on seeds, wild roots, small animals and fish, and even insects for food. Their lifestyle is simple, (or just plain barbaric to the Argonauts). Most of them have never had the luxury of postponing a meal until they are hungry.

The Humboldt River, mean as it might seem to the wagon travelers, is the source of much of their livelihood. The annual migration of thousands of people and animals down this frail lifeline is a disaster to them. They are cut off from the river for weeks by the migration, and they must watch helplessly as their food supply is destroyed by the invading horde of hungry people and animals.

They have been mistreated by the wagon people from the very beginning. Few dare approach a camp to trade or beg or steal. They fight for survival in the only way they can. Without arms or horses, they cannot openly attack the invaders. But they can steal his animals for food. And if the animals are too well guarded at night, they pepper them with small arrows, knowing the wounded animals will eventually weaken and be abandoned to die, at which time they will provide food for the Indian. Even stolen animals are killed rather than allowed to fall back into the hands of pursuing pioneers. The travelers have never before heard of an Indian who would steal a horse to eat rather than ride.

So, our journey down the Humboldt during the heat of August becomes even more debilitating. Our innocent devastation of the river means double guards every night—a further drain on our waning strength. Our surviving animals, ever more precious to us, continue to weaken, drop and perish from the rigors of our journey. And now we are in real danger of losing them to theft or arrows. Our night guards, at least, are also in peril from the flights of small arrows that can come at any time. We curse the Dreaded Digger.

This is not a romantic battle. In our ignorance of its causes, it will never occur to us to call it a battle. We will recall only thieving harassment. But it *is* a battle. Though we rarely see our enemy, he is there and he is hungry.

It is with relief that we finally pull into what will be called "Lassen's Meadow," (today Rye Patch Reservoir, between Lovelock and Winnemucca). We will rest a day to "recruit" our animals, before we make our final run to the sink and away from the Dreaded Diggers.

TO THE SINK

The trek down the Humboldt through Nevada's deserts is boring, and debilitating.

The people who will follow us in 1849 and 1850 will pay a terrible price during this part of their journey, but in 1848 we have not yet overgrazed the grass and stand a pretty good chance of getting through with both our wagons and our animals.

For the first time, we meet a train heading east. They are members from the former Mormon Battalion that went to California during the war with Mexico. After wintering in California, they are heading home to Salt Lake City. We finally get first-hand information of what lies ahead on the trail. They have explored and opened a new route over the Sierra, which they recommend to us. They also claim to have been witness to the discovery of gold we heard rumored in Fort Hall. We accept their story with a grain of salt, suspecting a little leg-pulling in retaliation for former (and continuing) persecutions.

We continue down the Humboldt to where it finally ceases to be a river and just "sinks" into the desert in big, miserable, swampy, alkali ponds. About a year from now, in 1849, Randall Fuller will say this about our route:

> ...*the grass poor and willow for fuel.... The water is very rily in this river and warm and a good deal of alchaly in it and hardly fit to drink and groes wors as we get down torg the sink. The fase of the earth looks as if it has ben burnt up the top of the earth looks like ashes and when the dust is a fling a man will al most suficat with it. The contry up and down this river is inhabet by the tribe of root diger indans these indans are vary (?) to lived beings, and go necked and are vary trobelsom to the emageantes in steling thair stock as they are travelling a through thair contry and if they cetch a man a lone they will kill him.*

Old Randall can't spell a lick, but he explains things real good!

Our critters are weak. Even Prince, the family dog, is doing poorly. He usually beats the heat by trotting along under our high wagon—in the shade. But the earth is still hot, and finally his paws get so raw that we have pity and let him ride. He is twice lucky. In many other trains he would have either been shot or eaten by now. Everyone else walks to help the oxen.

Now we have to make a choice: Do we cross the Forty

Desert west to the Truckee, the "old" route to California via Donner Pass, or do we follow Mr. Chiles south to the Carson River and the new route the Mormons told us about? The very name "Donner" gives us pause. We choose to follow Mr. Chiles.

We lighten our load yet again. Not much remains to throw away. We have but little flour and bacon, and lucky to have it. Kegs and trunks and the last of the heavy furniture go by the wayside. We have left a trail of junk behind for over 1500 miles, but this is near the last of it.

As we look ahead to crossing the Forty Mile Desert, we know we will have to make some hay for the animals and carry it along part way. We also need to take a little water, but it is hard to imagine the animals are strong enough to pull very much heavy water. This is a major quandary. Do we abuse our weary animals by making them pull heavy water, or abuse them by taking no water at all?

On one thing we are agreed. We will keep our tent. We *are* a married couple, after all.

THE FORTY MILE DESERT

W e are in a sump. Anywhere else it would be a swamp. The Humboldt River has been our lifeline across the desert, but it has turned sickly and lies dying in a mire of alkali ponds and sloughs.

Our choice is forty miles to the Truckee River or forty miles to the Carson River. We have opted for the Carson and prepare as best we can for the twenty hour trek—twenty hours if our wretched animals can keep anything like their normal pace. We take some little of the bad water available and make some hay to bait the stock part way through. We finally jump off late in the afternoon, hoping that travel by night will somehow conserve our poor oxen.

Next year the 49ers will not have so "easy" a time on the Forty Mile Desert, and it will become a true horror in 1850 when 45,000 souls make the trek and leave behind them thousands of dead animals and abandoned wagons. One 1850 diary claims to have counted over 9,700 dead animals and 3,000 lost wagons. Rescue parties were sent from Sacramento and The Diggings to help. A tent community called "Rag Town" grew on the banks of the Carson, occupied by speculators, traders, gamblers, scavengers and others drawn by the plight of the immigrants. Certainly they helped the Argonauts with their expensive supplies and aid. More certainly, they "helped themselves."

The diaries describe the ordeal. Randall Fuller, crossing in 1849, tells how he sent a man ahead on horseback to bring back water and what happened when he returned:

> *He met us about four miles from the river and relieved us with something more precious than gold...when I told the other men that the water had come they began to cry like little children....*

Later, at the river, he twice noted it was so hot in the desert that matches would ignite if placed on the burning sand. He also wrote:

> *The emigrants ariven hourly acrost the burning desert some of them losing all of thair animals and haf to foot it in, almost chocked to death for water...some crossing the desert become crazy.*

But, that is another time. After we work our way out of the brackish sloughs and muck holes near the sink, we pull steadily all night. Daylight finds us barely halfway. We rest our exhausted animals, give what water we have, bait them with our meagre store of hay. To rest too long is to trifle with disaster. We move out again and find the road has taken another diabolic turn. It is turning to sand. It is very heavy going, heaping yet another cruelty on our poor beasts.

In late afternoon the green cottonwoods on the Carson's banks come into view. We unyoke the oxen and begin driving them to water and grass, promising our families we will return tomorrow with the oxen refreshed to rescue wagons and kin.

And so we conquer the Forty Mile Desert. The greatest physical feat of our journey is still to come, but crossing the Forty Mile Desert will forever remain first in our memories as our greatest accomplishment. Never again will we be so hot, so tired, so weak, so hungry, so dispirited, so desperate.

In years to come, when the 49ers who will follow us gather to sing the parodies and songs of the Gold Rush, we will join in with special gusto on this verse of Sweet Betsy From Pike:

> They soon reached the desert, where Betsy gave out,
>   And down in the sand she lay rolling about,
> While Ike, half distracted, looked on with surprise,
>   Saying, "Betsy, get up, you'll get sand in your eyes."

But *we* did it! Forget that Elephant!

ON TO THE SIERRA

The Carson River is beautiful—clear, sweet, cold. After our desert ordeal, we take a few days to recruit the cattle and ourselves. The women and the bachelors get at their laundry, and soon cover all the bushes and small trees near our camp with drying clothing of every sort. (In later years, some will say that this is the real reason the area is called "Rag Town"). Many of us will bathe, though a few men will brag they haven't been out of their britches since we left the Missouri.

We move west along the river, and we meet our next discovery with what might be called stoic resignation: we have to abandon the river and cross The Twenty-Six Mile Desert! We know we can do it, but we wish we could ask someone "Why?" This grueling trek puts us into the Carson Valley proper and right beside the towering Sierra not far from the future site of Carson City.

Now we follow river and mountains through the

beautiful but odd combination of sagebrush and lush, watered meadows that make up this valley. We have the good luck to bag two doves and a sage hen. We add these to the trout we have caught and enjoy our best meal in weeks. Three day's travel bring us to *The Canyon*.

The distance from Woodfords to Hope Valley is only about five miles. It is the "longest five miles" of the trip and will take an entire, long day. There is no trail except a couple of crude bridges built by the Mormons earlier this summer when they opened the route. The river is the trail. It is narrow, steep, and full of boulders. It seems impossible to take a wagon through. In 1849 and 1850, abandoned and wrecked wagons abounded here. Only the Forty Mile Desert took a bigger toll on wagons.

In 1850, David Wooster wrote:

> *At the entrance of Big Kanyon, I think I saw the ruins of more than a hundred wagons and carriages. Emigrants fondly hope to take their wagons quite to the Gold Region, till they get here; but now the roaring of the river as it dashes down its rocky channel, the snow banks, and frightful precipices and sidling rocky road, and the three crossings of Kanyon River appall them....*

Another report:

> *...all the loose rocks and debris thrown together at the bottom, thro' which flows or rather leaks a mountain stream, with here and there patches of scanty soil, bearing*

loftey pines 4 and 5 ft in diameter amongst the rocks, and sometimes up steep hills loaded wagons had to pass in places where loose cattle could hardly keep their feet.

The turns are so sharp that only one team can be yoked. At times we have to unhitch the teams and turn the wagons with manual labor. It is a devastatingly exhausting day. Our reward comes late in the afternoon when we break out into a handsome valley of sage and grass—Hope Valley.

Well named.

MOUNTAIN MISERY

You must think we are joshing you. Only a few days back, we crossed the onerous Forty Mile Desert and truly feared some might perish before we were safe on the banks of the Carson River. Then, within the week, we had to conquer *The Canyon*—"The longest five miles of the journey."

That was only yesterday. Today we have pulled across Hope Valley to a small tarn called Red Lake, at the base of the First Pass. Now we stare up at a rock wall that is "the most dreaded ascent" of our entire journey. Some call it The Devil's Ladder. Later it will be simply Red Lake Grade, a descent of Carson Spur.

Trail life is bizarre. Not too many days back it was so hot that matches would flash of their own accord if dropped on the hot sand for any time. Last night we had a snow squall, and there was thick ice on the bucket this morning!

We "noon" at Red Lake and have time to think of the debt we owe the Mormons who opened this trail only weeks ago. The time they spent in "making road" and building crude bridges for their wagons has made it possible for us to get this far on this new route. Of course, they were going *down* hill. The route *up* hill was pioneered short days ago by the large train of Joseph Chiles that precedes us. They made road, too.

In the early afternoon, we attack the Devil's Ladder. Total distance is less than a mile, but it is impossible for us to attempt it in the usual fashion. It is so steep, so slippery, so full of obstructions, so sidling, so winding that we are stymied after the first hundred rods. We unload our remaining provisions and goods and pack them to the top of the grade. We move ahead with empty wagons, but soon find areas where the animals can't keep their footing on the slick granite. Unhitched, many fall to their knees and even crawl in crossing. Once the animals have footing, we must carry long chains back to the wagons so they can be pulled farther up the spur. Each time we stop for rest or to reposition our stock, we must block the wheels and snub ropes around the nearest trees to keep our wagons from falling backward.

In this manner we conquer the first pass. We didn't know it was still in us to take on such a chore. It is dark when we finally fall into our blankets, dinner hardly tasted.

Can Donner Pass possibly be tougher than this?

WEST PASS

It is the first week of September, in the Year of Our Lord, 1848. We are a family of four and we have crossed the continent by wagon. Our trip is nearly ended. We have crossed the endless Great Plains, climbed the Rocky spine of America, endured the arid and austere Great Basin and, toughest of all, survived the merciless Forty Mile Desert.

In truth, we are now in the midst of our sternest test. We are cresting the fearful eastern scarp of the Sierra Nevada. First we conquered The Canyon. Then, we pushed and crawled and toted until we topped The Devil's Ladder. Making our way through a beautiful meadow between two small lakes (later Caples Lake, then Twin Lakes, today Caples Lake again), we now take on The Pass.

It is six miles to the summit. We will then be at an altitude of over 9,500 feet—2,000 feet higher than friendly South Pass, which saw us easily over the

Rockies. It is the highest point of our trek, the highest pass regularly used by the wagon trains.

The first three miles are through timber. Then we are above the trees and find the trail so sidling that the men have to heave against the wagons to keep them from tipping and we require double teams the last two miles. Finally we hit a field of perpetual snow, hard as ice, and break our way to the top!

And there, we behold California at last! A later immigrant said,

> The new world of California bursts at once upon our impatient sight. Another: Nearly exhausted (men & animals) we reached the top—the highest point of the Sierra Nevada mountains, called the Backbone. Stopping we looked around & here is a view too magnificently grand and wildly romantic for me to attempt to describe....

The view extends over an area 200 miles by 500 miles. The desert, so recently conquered, can be clearly discerned. Before us we see the mountains we must descend and the great valley beyond. Distant mountains rob us of our first view of the Pacific Ocean. At least ten mountain lakes are in view, including the one that will be called Tahoe.

We are not so tired or so jaded as to not be stunned by the view. In truth, it will never leave our minds. We rejoice at the sights and brag that we stand upon "the Elephant's backbone."

Reality returns. We move down the mountain to a rocky valley and camp. There is no map to tell us otherwise; to us it will always be our *first camp in California!*

TRAGEDY SPRINGS

We have taken our wagon over the Elephant's Backbone (Carson Pass, or more accurately, West Pass), and made our first camp in California. Anxious to leave the mountains behind, we move down the trail, noting a large lake on our right (Silver Lake). We cross a nice meadow and come to a spring.

The Trail sobers us again by what we find: a grave, marked by a large pile of rocks. The inscription carved on a nearby fir tree tells the entire story: *"To the memory of Daniel Browett, Ezra H. Allen, and Henderson Cox, who were supposed to have been murdered and buried by Indians on the night of the twenty-seventh of June, A.D. 1848."*

These were the scouts of the Mormon party we met in the desert short weeks ago. The Mormons touted this new route to us and told of their loss at Tragedy Springs. Back in June, three of their number, anxious to get home to family in Salt Lake City, volunteered to scout ahead for the best wagon route. They never returned. On July 19, the train reached the spring and found evidence of a camp with signs of struggle. There was also an ominous mound of fresh earth. Fearing the worst, they dug it up to a shocking sight. The murdered scouts lay naked in the one hole, two face down and Allen on his back with an ax wound in his head. The victims were robbed of their guns, horses and clothing, but not their gold. Bloody and broken arrows were found in the grave and in the vicinity. They were judged to have died their second night out—June 27, 1848. After a proper burial, stones were piled high on the grave to protect them from animals, and the tree inscribed.

Indians again! We had little trouble with the warrior Sioux or Blackfoot of the Plains, but the despised "Digger" of the desert nearly did us in. Now in California at last, we find ourselves at a grave barely 60 days old that puts a lie to the claim California Indians are all placid and docile.

The west slope of the Sierra is much easier going than the east side. We continue to be astonished at the size of the pine trees in this new country. Twenty feet in girth is common! We relish the sound of the wind in the trees—something we have missed for many hundreds of miles. We make camp at Leek Springs above Camp Creek. It offers few leeks, a lot of weeds, and the feeling we must be nearly "there."

THE GOLD MINER

Two days from Leek Springs we meet our first gold miner! Our anxious company overwhelms the poor fellow and he is almost devoured by our attention and questions. Not only does he offer our first fresh news in weeks, we crave the story of gold. The more he talks, the more importance gold assumes.

First to the news. The war with Mexico that had discouraged pioneers from coming to California is definitely over. The peace treaty is already signed. The military governor of California is General Richard B. Mason, but he is in trouble because his men are deserting the army for the goldfields. Old Zack Taylor is running for president. And gold is here for the finding!

Our new friend tells us gold was first found in January and by spring, the main towns of California were almost deserted of able-bodied men as the stampede for the gold fields began. Crews are deserting their ships; farmers are abandoning their fields; doctor, lawyer and merchant are forsaking desk and counter to the search for gold. He guessed there might be 2000 Americans and as many others in on the search already and reckoned that people would rush to California by the thousands in '49!

This intoxicating news leaves our bedraggled and trail-worn group of argonauts in absolute awe. We listen like babes, each with his mouth agape. Never did such a thought occur to any of us when we crossed the Missouri in May. The first news at Fort Hall left us dubious. The confirmation by the Mormon party we met in the desert excited us, but we dared not believe what we were now hearing. We have proof in hand, as our generous friend freely passes out samples from his heavy poke. He assures us there is plenty more, but it might be best to wait for the first rains since the diggings are pretty dry now.

Wait? We are already addicted. We want to dig gold *now!* We talk far into the night, asking, learning. We soak up amazing stories of $500 earned in one day, thousands in a week! Apparently there is no crime since there is gold enough for all who will work but a little.

We finally turn in for some fidgety sleep. *We are only a day away!* Before breakfast, most of the single men are already gone. They are forgiven. Tomorrow will be *our* day!

GOLD FEVER

Our little wagon train is trying to speed down the mountains to the waiting goldfields, but oxen have a built-in governor that peaks out at about two and half miles per hour. Considering our weary critters have been on the trail for four months and covered almost two thirds of the continent, we are lucky to make that. Only because the wagons are now nearly empty and the trail is mostly down hill makes even this progress feasible. We begin to see signs of prospecting, but after twenty miles we are forced to make yet another camp short of our new goal.

Finally, we find ourselves moving into the "diggings". We are all excited about the gold, but the ladies are also disappointed. They have saved one pair of shoes, one special ribbon, one clean apron, one new bonnet for their first appearance in civilization in four months. They had hoped to stop and try to wash and cream away four months of sun and wind burn before showing themselves to polite society again. It wouldn't have worked, you know. It will take a few months of pampering to do away with that look that says you have just come off the trail.

So, instead of our planned triumphal entry into Sutter's, we gradually come into the Diggings. Curious men run up to the wagons to trade news and to look at the first ladies most of them have seen in several months—trail worn though they may be.

Information comes to us almost faster than we can comprehend. We are approaching Weber Creek. Gold was first found here in late Spring by a German ranchero named Captain Charles Weber. After discovery, he returned to the Valley and formed the *Stockton Mining Company*. They returned to mine and set up a store. They hired local Indians and trained them in mining. The store stocks blankets, silver coins, and other trade goods to pay the Indian crew for gold nuggets and dust. At first gold could be taken with teaspoons and hunting knives. Men used wash basins and Indian baskets. Now you have to dig and pan. Cradles are also used to wash gold, but it is still the dry season and there is not enough water right where you need it. The miners are awaiting the fall rains.

Men are living in tents, brush lean-tos, or under simple shades made from canvas or blankets. The "store" turns out to be no more than a brush hut. We have arrived just as it is getting ready to close up shop for good. Weber's Indians have found gold on the

Stanislaus River and most of the miners have moved to these new southern diggings. Hundreds of pounds of gold have been taken from this camp in a few short months, and it is almost abandoned already! Maybe 200 men remain in the area. Those that stayed are averaging about an ounce a day.

An ounce a day! That is $16.00—a month's wages for some of us back in the States! We make camp and we take lessons and we start digging and we find our first gold! And then we dig some more. From dawn to dusk we can't stop. Digging, digging, how can we stop? We have gold fever.

Is there a cure?

FAMILY

Our little wagon train is no more. Less than one-hundred miles from our goal we have scattered. Some are mining here at Weber Creek, some have moved over to Diamond Springs, others to Old Dry Diggings that—for good reason—will be called Hangtown next year. Some have gone on to Sacramento and others to the Southern Mines. Little did we realize four months and 1900 miles back that we would plod down these mountains into a miracle! Gold! Gold for everyone!

I don't remember the exact instant that I was cured of Gold Fever. If I had stopped digging long enough to shave, a look in the mirror would have cured me sooner. But reality did return. I looked at my children and suddenly realized they had a touch of scurvy from bad diet and were skinny as rails. Where were they going to school? For the first time in days I looked at my loyal wife and saw the miserable wagon and camp that she was trying to make into a home for our children and this wild–eyed miner. Finally, I looked at myself, my state of health and the madness that had gripped me. It was finally obvious that this was not the life for a family. The rainy season would soon be here, bringing water to the miners but agony to my loved ones.

Only the dog and the other animals have improved. Except the need of new shoes, my horse hasn't looked so good since we left the Prairies, the oxen and the cow are getting sleek again and I daily turn down big offers for my oxen as meat animals. But you don't part from old, loyal friends so easily. Mountain, desert, heat and storm, they plodded through it all without protest. We are surely here because of them and we mourn the loss of the two dead on the trail. There is no doubt no one ever loved dumb animals more than we love these patient, enduring oxen.

Except for a small poke of gold dust, we are back where we were on the trail. What to do? We are farmers and we came to California in search of good soil, good climate, and to escape disease—especially the ague. Where do we start?

One option is to go to San Francisco. They say it is a boom town with easy money to be made. Another is the town of Sacramento, growing on the river next to Sutter's Fort. It was our original destination. Finally, before he closed up shop and left, the last storekeeper at Weber's Store told us that the Captain had sold out his mining interests and returned to his rancho in the valley to tend to the town he had started called Stockton. He said Weber is so anxious to attract good, solid settlers that he is even giving away town lots to those who will build and stay. And he offers good terms to those who want to buy land to farm.

We are in no mood to gamble. Maybe it is the letdown from my mining "spree." It is suddenly paramount that we get settled before winter and take care of our family. Stockton sounds like the best bet. Captain Weber doesn't know it, but a trail-worn farm wagon, a family of four, six oxen, a milch cow, a horse, and a shaggy dog are about to become his next "solid" settlers.

THE END OF THE TRAIL

Finding our way from Weber's Diggings to his new town of Stockton is not as easy as it sounds. There are no roads, only the pack trails that have just been broken in this past Spring following the news of gold. Except for the last few months, the Sierra foothills were never settled and rarely explored. We are aided somewhat by following the tracks left by the Stockton Mining Company, which blazed a trail of sorts for supplies brought to Weberville and Weber's Diggings from Weber's rancho headquarters at Stockton.

The countryside still teems with game, especially deer. We find antelope as we move out of the hills and later, near the marshes, see small elk, called "Tule Elk" here. Grizzly bear also abound and we take great care to avoid contact with them, just as we did in the Rockies. The California Grizzly is said to be bigger and fiercer than any animal we have yet encountered.

Missing from this experience are Indians. We saw

some in the diggings, and we see sign of old villages along our way. We later learn that epidemics in 1833 and 1845 decimated the local population. If gold had been discovered only four years sooner, the Indian would have been a big factor in the Gold Rush story. We found at Tragedy Springs they are not necessarily a docile people, and now we hear that they kept the Spanish and Mexican Governments at bay for decades, the San Joaquin River being the dividing line between Hispanic and Indian-controlled territories.

We trail through marvelous groves of huge oak trees and are puzzled how they grow where everything is so dry! We have had rain only once since we left the high mountains and the occasional travelers we meet tell us it is common for no rain to fall between May and October. How do you grow a crop without summer rain?

At last we approach the only settlement we have yet seen in California—the village of Stockton. There is one wooden house, one adobe house, one married American couple, and bustling activity as canvas structures are built for shelter and commerce. Supplies arrive from San Francisco by whale boat and are readied for the mines. Wages are sixteen dollars per day. Some miners are coming in from the mountains in anticipation of winter and others are headed for "dry diggings" in anticipation of water at last.

No churches, no schools, little government, no families, saloons going up right and left—we are in a frontier settlement we can understand. We are on the ground floor for the first time in our lives. We have decided that second-hand gold is as good as new. Stockton is now "home."

"Cap'n Weber, sir, we are a family of four newly-arrived by wagon from the States by way of your diggings. We have chosen Stockton as our new home. Now, about that offer of free land...."

1848

Serendipity! That is just about the only word to describe the choice of 1848 for a trek by wagon train from the Missouri to the San Joaquin. The year 1848 was originally selected because it is the last true year of exploration by the migrants. It is the year the Carson and Lassen Routes open and every change after this will be of minor significance in comparison. It is also the last year before the Gold Rush changes the trail forever. It can be called the last "pristine" year.

Serendipity comes into play when it finally dawns that if this train follows Joseph Chiles over Carson Pass, we are going to "fall into" the early Gold Rush and the persona of Charles Weber, founder of Stockton, California.

In regards to the California end of the trail, the story of Tragedy Springs is absolutely on point. That a stray miner would pass out "samples" from his poke is in character with the nature of the Gold Rush as it is in '48. This first summer is unlike any other. Most of the men in California are in the Diggings and most of them will actually find gold, unlike the hordes of next year. Crime is not a problem this first summer. There truly seems to be gold for all who will but work a little, and so there is no need to rob or steal.

The contrast with '49 will be remarkable. As quickly as men can cross the Plains, 'round the Horn, jump the Isthmus, or sail in from Hawaii or Chili, the world will truly "rush in," as one author aptly puts it, and California and the Diggings will never again be the same. Not only will the "easy pickin's" be gone, but the criminal element will join up while many a good, young, "Christian gentleman" from Back East, separated from the puritan restraints of home and society for the first time, will go on a monumental binge of booze, cigars, faro cards, bear and bull fights, and fandangos.

Our arrival in '48 allows us to witness the death throes of Hispanic Northern California. It was a fragile culture. After all, there had not been a single Spanish resident in the Mother Lode or the Great Valley during Spain's long tenure from 1542 through 1822. Only a handful of the estimated 15,000 Californios edged into these areas during Mexico's short reign from 1822 to 1846. They were overwhelmed by the Gold Rush.

We observe the last pitiful stand of the native Indians. Their teeming thousands had already been decimated by the plagues of 1832 and the small pox epidemic of 1939. The San Joaquin County census tells the story: 379 Indian residents in 1850, forty-one in 1860, and a sad five in 1879.

We are spectator to the still untouched wonders of California's immense strata of big game, wildlife, and forests, before the deluge of '49. We will be the generation that remembers the tule elk herds, the grizzly, the magnificent salmon runs.

Finally, our 1848 trek puts us in the venue of Charles M. Weber, a remarkable pioneer, now little remembered outside the city he founded. And it lets us in on the "ground floor" of the founding of his City of Stockton, California.

Serendipity. That's the word for it.

SUGGESTED READING

Trail literature abounds and continues to grow at a great rate. Newly discovered diaries and journals are published each year. This small list is meant only to whet the appetite of the potential trail buff.

The California Trail

Stewart, George R. *The California Trail*. N.Y. McGraw-Hill 1962

Hunt, Thomas H. *Ghost Trails To California.* Palo Alto, American West 1974

Hill, William E. *The California Trail Yesterday and Today*. Boulder, Pruett 1986

Western Trails — General

Paden, Irene D. *The Wake Of The Prairie Schooner.* Patrice Press reprint.

Unruh, John D., Jr. *The Plains Across.* Chicago, University of Illinois Press 1982

Mattes, Merrill J. *The Great Platte River Road,* Lincoln, Nebraska State Historical Soc. 1969

Works Based On Diaries

Stewart, George R. *Ordeal By Hunger, The Story of the Donner Party*, Bison Edition, Lincoln, University of Nebraska Press 1986

Holiday, J.S. *The World Rushed In.* N.Y. Simon and Schuster 1981

ACKNOWLEDGEMENTS

"When you steal from one author, it's plagiarism; if you steal from many, it's research."
Wilson Mizner

It is with some embarrassment that I must confess to the greater crime of ignorance as to many of the sources that were tapped during the composition of this series.

As noted in the *Foreword*, these pieces were generally written quite spontaneously, with little consideration of where the lore originated. Further, the informal style does not lend itself to footnotes or careful documentation. It was always meant to be a generic and popular treatment of trail life, and never intended for general publication.

It is certain that credit must go to George R. Stewart's *California Trail*, which is my personal favorite general treatment of the subject. In fact, I see his hand in almost every broad discussion of the California Trail.

More specifically, the extensive quotes from Randall Fuller's wonderful diary were taken from the *Overland Journal*, Volume 6, Number 4, 1988. (The bad spelling of one short quote was altered to aid the flow of the story).

The *Doctor On The Trail* episode was suggested by a paper of Dr. Peter D. Olch, also from the *Overland Journal*, Volume 6, No. 1 1988. Commentary and conclusions, however, are strictly my own.

Sincere apologies to any serious trail scholar whose specific work may be evident but not properly cited. The oversight is unintentional.

Please note the special sketches and graphics of Sharon Dell'Osso, and the distinctive cover design of Alex Roessler. Great work! Thanks also to Larey Smith, who did the map, and to Lydia Kim for her patient lay-out work.

The F.O.C. Darley lithograph *Emigrants Crossing The Plains* is from the collection of old friend Hugh Hayes.

Special thanks must go to Sylvia Sun Minnick of *Heritage West Books,* who insisted this collection be published and then did it. She was a fan from the very beginning.

Finally, appreciation is due my patient wife Alice, who muttered hardly at all when work on this series postponed all manner of outings and good times.

The Author

A life-long history buff, Bob Shellenberger takes naturally to the story of the wagon trains. His interest has always been in the story of the middling pioneers and how they met the dare of their way of life despite personal ignorance, imperfections, and inadequacies. The trail tested all the argonauts.

He is currently president of the San Joaquin County Historical Society. His other affiliations include the Stockton Corral of Westerners (past sheriff), the Oregon-California Trails Association, East Contra Costa County Historical Society, and the California Historical Society. (He claims dues are his major contribution to history).

A 1952 graduate of San Jose State University, and a fourth-generation Californian, he has lived in Stockton since 1952. Currently, he is serving his sixth consecutive term as San Joaquin County Assessor.